Break the Cycle: A Personal Journey of Overcoming OCD

Lee williams

Published by Lee williams, 2024.

While every precaution has been taken in the preparation of this book, the publisher assumes no responsibility for errors or omissions, or for damages resulting from the use of the information contained herein.

BREAK THE CYCLE: A PERSONAL JOURNEY OF OVERCOMING OCD

First edition. January 11, 2024.

Copyright © 2024 Lee williams.

ISBN: 979-8224919505

Written by Lee williams.

Table of Contents

Real life- that's what I am talking about here, not a definition in a book or website. I want to put across my personal thoughts and experiences that span across fifteen years. I started writing this when I was twenty seven and now, at the ripe old age of forty three, I'm finishing it. So you'll find there are sections of the story that switch between my past and the present. I'm not trained or an expert, but I am someone who has lived in depth with OCD.

. . . .

I HAVE SUFFERED FROM OCD and have been in relationships with people who have also suffered with this mental illness. Therefore, I feel that I might be able to help, even if it is just enlightening on certain facts or raising awareness that you aren't alone out there.

. . . .

I RECENTLY POSTED A letter in an OCD forum talking about how I have lived with others suffering from OCD and how this is just as difficult as having OCD yourself. To my amazement, I got over twenty replies straight away. Most of these were from those who have friends and loved ones gripped by this mental illness.

I noticed a lot of desperation in those letters. Like me, these people were at their wits end; not knowing what to do, where to turn or how to help the ones they loved. I replied to each email personally, talking about their problems and suggesting ways to help and I've included some of these letters at the end of the book.

. . . .

IT'S EASY TO LOOK ON the internet and get a definition of OCD but in my opinion these definitions have their limitations. Often, they don't really help, seeming a little impersonal and even scary and it's one of the reasons I decided to write this. I wanted to try and shine a light to show there are people like you out there, the sufferers of OCD and those who are close to the sufferers.

First things first, what is OCD? It is short for **obsessive-compulsive disorder**. The International OCD foundation describes it as, *a mental health disorder that affects people of all ages and walks of life and occurs when a person gets caught in a cycle of obsessions and compulsions. Obsessions are unwanted, intrusive thoughts, images, or urges that trigger intensely distressing feelings. Compulsions are behaviours an individual engages in to attempt to get rid of the obsessions and/or decrease his or her distress.*

. . . . .

OCD TAKES ON MANY FORMS but the distressing thoughts or images that can affect sufferers physically and mentally are usually caused by repetitive tasks and compulsions. On one level, it's like when a song gets lodged in your head. You just can't shake it; it plays over and over in your mind like a broken record. Over and over until it starts to drive you mad.

. . . . .

THE REPETITIVE SONG is a lot like OCD, you are plagued by the same thoughts and repeat actions, to the point where you become fully consumed both mentally and physically. You know it is all in your mind but can't get rid of those false beliefs.

. . . . .

IF YOU HAVE OCD, IT is highly likely you're already familiar with these definitions, but I'm writing this to go beyond the defined '*textbook*' and to look in detail at *real life situations*. You may know a friend who has been engulfed by obsessive thoughts. You might, like I did, also live with someone who is trapped in its cycle.

Lee, I am twenty-seven years old (*twenty-seven at the time of writing but now forty three and adding to this book*) and from the northeast of England.

. . . .

GROWING UP I WAS A shy kid. I suffered from terrible acne throughout my teenage years which affected me in quite a dramatic way. As I lurched into those years my acne decided to get much worse. Looking back now as a grown man I can see this is where I really started to struggle with my appearance and when the first signs of a very personal battle with OCD started to show up in my life.

. . . .

I'M GRATEFUL TO HAVE had an amazing relationship with my grandparents and most weekends would spend time with them. My grandma had a makeup case that she'd carry around everywhere, using it to freshen up her face from time to time. On one occasion it had been left out and I couldn't help but look through the makeup. I felt so desperate about the state of my skin that I took some and applied it to cover up my acne. It must have looked really odd to my grandparents, their teenage grandson emerging with a contoured face! I remember them noticing and my grandad's voice carrying in from the second room, "Is Lee wearing your makeup? Why is he doing that?" I was mortified and felt too embarrassed to tell them the real reason I had done it.

. . . .

FROM THAT DAY ON I never used my grandma's makeup again, but I did find a concealer stick from the chemist instead. It was yet another embarrassing situation for me, a teenage boy in the nineties buying makeup. But I figured it was less embarrassing than the humiliation of my own grandparents watching me walk around covered in blusher dots too brown for my face. My grandma favoured a deep, almost mahogany coloured tone of makeup and I was quite light skinned, so the overall effect was to kind of make me look cheetah-like. No wonder they seemed a little shocked as I walked into the room where they sat, but this was the lengths OCD had pushed me to.

• • • •

OVER TIME I GOT MORE inventive about using other methods to hide my skin, one of these was to wear a scarf around my face. I'd check the weather forecast ahead and if I saw it was going to be a bit cloudy I'd be happy as it meant I could wrap up in the scarf. I'd still do this, even in the stifling heat, walk about sweating in my scarf. The discomfort was worth it as far as I was concerned as at least people couldn't see my skin. It allowed me to hide in plain sight I guess.

• • • •

DURING THOSE TEEN YEARS I started to really suffer from overbearing, negative self awareness. I would constantly look in the mirror, constantly check my skin and generally avoid the gaze of others.

• • • •

I BECAME OBSESSED WITH my appearance and in particular, with cleaning my face. It got to the point where I would avoid going to college to try and hide away from people. In the mornings, I'd take the bus in but would rarely get off when it arrived. I'd sit for ages past the college stop and go for long walks in the countryside instead. This was my way of avoiding people. It was lonely but on the plus side, I became fitter from all the miles of trekking and as far as my parents were concerned, I went to college every day. Little did they know I was bunking off, walking around on my own carrying about this great sadness because I had to hide away from others. I'd self isolated as a way of trying to make myself feel better. OCD did this.

Is OCD doing something similar to you? Do you self isolate as a way of protecting yourself?

I really did feel like I was something to be ashamed of. That was what my brain was telling me anyway. It's amazing what that self-sabotaging voice in your head can do to you isn't it. The voice that tells you, '*You aren't quite good enough*' or, '*you're going to fail again so why try*.' It's really difficult to ignore this voice but to progress we need to develop a louder inner one that reassures us '*it's going to be ok, we can do it.*'

Self loathing and obsession took me away from life. I didn't want to participate in it and kind of gave up, taking this sense of helplessness with me everywhere I went. The whole episode left its mark and still, even today I have lingering issues around how I look and how others perceive me.

• • • •

I CAN ALMOST PINPOINT this mindset to a very specific OCD behaviour. As a young man, I would carry around a pocket mirror everywhere I went. I became obsessive about meticulously checking myself in it. Not to gaze adoringly at my face in some vain, Dorian Gray-esque way but to make sure my appearance was ok. When I peered into the mirror I was the same as I looked when I left the house, but I still needed to check, to make sure I was acceptable to other people. That internal voice was always whispering, '*do you look good enough?*,' and boy was it persistent. Even though I knew my behaviour was strange I would repeatedly ask, '*why am I doing this?*'. The urge to do it had overtaken me and I just couldn't stop. I was firmly in the clutches of obsession during those teen and early twenties years. OCD had a grip of me.

First Push (Into Life)

I finished college and had no idea what to do with my life. I felt alone and wrung out from years of hiding from people and almost hating the way I looked. I decided I needed to take another step forward even though it was painful, it was time to find some work and get into the real world.

· · · · ·

I WAS EIGHTEEN YEARS old and had kind of drifted into factory work for a year. When I was on shift, I fell into familiar patterns of isolating from others and carrying the mirror around in my pocket. I would seek out quiet corners on the factory floor and quickly take the mirror out so I could get a quick glance of my face, just to check. *'Just to check'* the little voice would tell me over and over again, in a way to almost convince me that what I was doing was normal, that it was ok to be doing this.

· · · · ·

IN THE END, I DECIDED factory work wasn't for me and needed more in my life, so guess what? I got a job in a nightclub of all places. At least it was dark in there and people couldn't see my skin as easily.

· · · · ·

THIS JOB WAS A BIG leap. I'd suffered and hid away throughout my adolescent years and was now, at the age of twenty, standing in a packed nightclub. It was a simple glass collecting job but it meant that I was on the move and didn't have to stand directly in front of people like the guys working on the bar. And I was careful to stick to my tried and tested tactic of hiding away from the gaze of others by collecting glasses from the darker corners of the club like some kind of vampire. Mwha ha ha haaaa.

• • • •

BUT THEN SOMETHING strange and unexpected happened. This vampire began to make a few friends and it helped me start to feel better about myself and life in general. I was still suffering with my skin, but I felt ok, like there was a light at the end of the tunnel.

• • • •

THIS IS WHEN I FIRST met a girl...

Zoe was like a ball of much needed fun being thrown into my life. She seemed alive and vibrant, a total polar opposite to how I had been over the last few years. I first bumped into her on a night out with mates from my glass collecting job when a friend announced she was bringing one of her pals, Zoe out with us. Straight away I was drawn to her bubbliness and even better, she appeared to like me which was a big WOW as I'd had such little luck with women due to being shy and my bad skin eroding away any confidence.

• • • •

THE NIGHT TURNED OUT to be a great laugh and Zoe wanted to see me again, so that's just what we did, we had another great time out and things naturally progressed. I remember her saying at one point that she could be normal around me, which made me think but I let it go. Zoe eventually explained she had this thing called OCD and that's when I started to live in her world. It was a world which turned out to be scary and very upsetting.

• • • •

GRADUALLY AND UNFORTUNATELY, OCD started to become a stronger and stronger part of mine and Zoe's relationship. One of the things I remember in particular was her obsession with the fireplace. Every night, she would sit in front of the gas fire for at least an hour after she had turned it off. Just sitting there by herself in the cold, staring at it intensely. I once asked her why she did it and her reply was numbly, *'I don't really know.'* Zoe knew deep down the fire was safe, but couldn't walk away, just in case it might still be on. At first, I would sit with her, to try and keep her company but it used to make things worse as focusing on the fire demanded one hundred percent of Zoe's attention. Me being there only served as a distraction from such a pressing task.

· · · ·

SO I'D LEAVE AND COME back fifteen minutes later. She'd still be sat staring intently at the fire, every so often compulsively flicking the switch back on and off again to ensure it was completely dead. Even after an hour of watching it, she still had to wait to be extra sure. It was the only thing that made her feel ok. It made her feel safe.

· · · ·

THIS CIRCULAR BEHAVIOUR often lasted for hours leaving her exhausted and upset. When she finally did leave the room, satisfied it was properly off, the compulsion to check would sometimes take over again, forcing her once more, to head back and look and starting the whole cycle again.

· · · ·

Do you know someone who suffers from an issue like this?
Caught in a cycle of obsession?
constantly checking to make sure something is locked or turned off
so that they can feel it's safe enough in their mind?
Have you asked them about this or why they do it?

· · · ·

IT MUST BE SO DISTRESSING for that person, *'trapped in the cycle'* that never ends but likewise, I know how upsetting it is for those who have to watch it re-play constantly from the side-lines. Looking on as the person you love goes round and round getting more stressed over what is basically a simple task to most people. Those close to the sufferer often end up feeling totally defeated as, much of the time, their offers of help are rejected or to make matters even worse, the person offering the help just gets screamed at. That's what used to happen to me and it would leave me utterly deflated and rejected.

•••••

I WANTED DESPERATELY to fix things for Zoe but being perfectly honest I didn't really know what to do, so my way of helping involved trying to make life as easy as possible. I would comply with what she wanted, I would go along with tasks such as showering multiple times a day just to try and alleviate the pressure on her.

•••••

LOOKING BACK, I CAN see this wasn't the best strategy. All I had become was an enabler by going along with it all and this served to justify Zoe's actions in her own mind. Being so young, I just acted without thinking but I was also acting out of love.

•••••

I HATED SEEING WHAT the illness was doing to Zoe and to us as a couple but every time I tried, I would keep getting screamed at, like it was me causing all this to happen. Eventually OCD eroded our relationship to the point of no return. I was only twenty one and just couldn't handle the intensity of it. I left the relationship defeated, almost destroyed and it took a long while to rebuild myself.

•••••

I WAS MENTALLY DRAINED and physically a shadow of my former self as I'd lost so much weight from all the stress and worry. I'm a natural fighter and this fighting spirit is what pushed me to keep trying to help Zoe, but after months and months of trying I felt like a punch-drunk boxer, confused by what had just happened to me.

L ike Zoe I know what it's like to be *trapped in the cycle*; it's exhausting and scary. A sufferer of OCD often feels the task they are performing on a loop is in some way critical to their life, like it will be the end of the world if they don't do it or finish it. Completion of the task in question brings with it some sense of relief, but it's usually short lived and the need to do it again, to satisfy that nagging inner voice, unfortunately soon reappears.

. . . .

I'VE HAD URGES IN THE past, to constantly check myself in the mirror and a few years later this was followed by washing my hair repeatedly. It felt like this was the most important thing in the world and would take up hours of the day. It made me feel bad, even ill, draining me of all my energy and resources. But please know, especially if you are feeling hopeless, that although it's hard to reprogram your mind away from these compulsions and repetitive behaviours it is very much possible.

. . . .

LATER IN TI IE BOOK I'LL talk about ways to help yourself and the people you care about, there's no quick fix with this sort of thing and mental illnesses are complicated. It takes time but the most important element is to acknowledge there is a problem, to take that first huge step.

. . . .

OTHER SYMPTOMS OF OCD can involve constantly rearranging objects. One that is particularly debilitating is called *counting*, which is where a person counts their footsteps. For example, their mind might tell them they are only allowed to walk ten steps to the car. They perceive something bad will happen if it's more or less steps and so not sticking to the ten becomes very distressing to the sufferer and usually means having to repeat the stepping many times over.

• • • •

YOU CAN SEE THIS *counting* in action during Episode 5, Season 4 of the **Big Bang Theory**, '*The Desperation Emanation*,' where Sheldon is counting his steps down the stairs. Although it looks comical to the viewer and yes his antics do draw laughter from the audience, they also highlight a classic way in which people become trapped in a cycle.

• • • •

AS SHELDON REACHES the bottom he's interrupted and because of this, feels he must start the cycle of counting again right from the beginning. Most people watching would find it amusing, putting it down to one of Sheldon's quirks, but what this really shows is a classic and very distressing OCD compulsion; counting for self-reassurance which follows a set routine until completed, no matter how long it takes.

• • • •

I'VE SEEN THIS FORM of OCD in action myself, a friend of mine had the very same problem. It would involve counting every step and repeating it obsessively until she got it right. We'd be in the street, walking together but with her head held down, eyes glued to the floor so that she could step over the cracks. All the while walking back to nervously recheck objects making sure they were '*safe*.' This type of behaviour is called 'checking' and involves different kinds of intrusive thoughts or fears.

• • • •

AS YOU CAN IMAGINE, it took us an exceptionally long time to get anywhere, and we looked pretty strange to passers-by. I became as stressed as she was because in those moments I was living in her world, following her along while she carried out the checks. I also found myself looking on the ground worrying if there was something that would catch her eye. I had to give constant reassurance (asking for this is a common symptom in sufferers) that the things she saw on the ground, like liquid or pieces of rubbish, were not a danger. Even after passing an object, she'd ask, '*is it ok?*' and I'd always reply with, '*yes, it's fine*' and nothing to worry about. Often, she'd turn around and go back to look at the object again, hence being 'trapped in the cycle.'

• • • •

THIS IS HOW A PERSON caught in OCD thinks; that *everything* is going to harm them. It is so hard to live in a person's OCD world but remember it's also ok to talk to others if you live with someone who has OCD. You are suffering just as much. I can say this, hand on heart as I've lived in both worlds, one as a sufferer and the other being with sufferers.

• • • •

I'VE ASKED MYSELF MANY times why my friend acted like she did and I believe her brain was telling her that something bad was going to happen to her or someone she loved if she didn't go back and check the cracks or objects. From being around people with OCD and in particular this 'checking or counting' behaviour, I made the link that they also suffered from high levels of anxiety. The anxiety seemed to make them hyper aware of their surroundings and focus on objects or things that caught their eye. Once this happened, the checking would be compounded further by overwhelming feelings of worry coming from that nagging inner voice, which urged if they didn't check correctly then bad things would happen.

• • • •

ANXIETY OCCURS FOR many reasons but I think a real danger point for increased anxious feelings linked to OCD can be in the teenage years. It's the time when your body is wildly changing, fuelled by hormones and you are more vulnerable to unrealistic ideals from society and social media. Ideals that champion misguided images of perfectionism as the way you should be. The ensuing anxiety from those formative years can fuel OCD and depression, and the *'counting and checking'* routine I've described offers relief to the sufferer, like a way of taking back control. The problem is, it's only a false control and one that often leads onto more forms of OCD.

• • • •

SO, ANXIETY IS A KEY issue that leads to all-consuming thoughts, thoughts like thinking that if you don't go back to check then something terrible is going to happen to yourself. In that person's mind it's a very real threat and this is what makes it such a mental trap, hence *'trapped in a cycle.'* It's a cycle that's extremely hard to break free from. It is also soul destroying, seeing an individual you care about reduced to going back and forth counting steps, stepping over cracks and focusing on objects as if they were poisonous.

• • • •

Does this all sound familiar to you?
Do you know a person who suffers like this?
Do you think you suffer like this?

• • • •

IF IT'S A YES TO ANY of these questions, then you are certainly not alone in such ways of acting and feeling but there are ways through it. There is a light, even if it may seem a dim and distant one. I'm a great believer in the power of words and some of the best writers put amazing emotion into words that can truly lift you.

This poem by Charles Bukowski offers self-determination in the face of life's hardships and implores the reader to take charge of their path and destiny even when things get tough. It urges you to transcend your struggles:

. . . .

The Laughing Heart
your life is your life
don't let it be clubbed into dank submission.
be on the watch.
there are ways out.
there is light somewhere.
it may not be much light but
it beats the darkness.
be on the watch.
the gods will offer you chances.
know them.
take them.
you can't beat death but
you can beat death in life, sometimes.
and the more often you learn to do it,
the more light there will be.
your life is your life.
know it while you have it.
you are marvellous
the gods wait to delight
in you.
Charles Bukowski

. . . .

FORTUNATELY, I HAVE never suffered from this type of OCD; counting or looking at objects on the floor but I can imagine doing such things. If I walk down the street and allow myself to fixate on the pavement, I quickly find myself stepping over the cracks, re-checking objects, counting steps. It can be scary and much easier than you think to fall down that rabbit hole.

One of the main reasons these behaviours can get such a firm stranglehold is because sufferers don't usually go to the doctor or even tell people about their problems, mainly because they're scared or embarrassed. I certainly know I was. It's all too easy to hide that part of you away, keep it a secret and use 'checking' as a means to gain some measure of control in your life, but it's false control and in a sense it's the OCD that is controlling you.

• • • •

HOW MANY PEOPLE OUT there suffer from OCD and hide it from friends and family? Have you ever seen a person acting in a way that does not seem quite right? Maybe you know someone? This is how it started with Zoe, I had no idea how much it had a grip on her life and by the time I knew, it was too late. I was all in and had totally trapped myself.

• • • •

I RECENTLY RECEIVED an email from a reader asking for advice about his friend whose behaviour was getting worse and worse:

• • • •

As a younger man my friend lived at home to care for his mum who had MS. He used to tell me how the responsibility of looking after her stressed him out so much that it gave him severe anxiety. This developed into OCD, which gradually got worse and worse. One year we went to Italy, and he couldn't eat any of the nice food for fear of contamination (this was before the pandemic). He would sit there just eating crisps and biscuits

*directly from the pack in front of us all, using the packet like
cutlery so he didn't have to touch any of it.*

I REPLIED THAT MAYBE all the pressure of looking after an ill parent
from an early age had affected him. I suggested talking to him openly;
sometimes you need to be a little direct with OCD and often skirting
around the subject doesn't help anybody.

. . . .

GETTING TREATMENT FOR the condition is a very big step and
needs a lot of support and understanding from the people around them.
Their bizarre behaviour might not make any sense to a non- sufferer and
can be frustrating, however for those struggling day to day with obsessive
compulsive disorder it's important not to forget that for them it is an
overriding and all-consuming mental issue.

University Years - Take 1

In 1998 I decided to be brave and apply for university. I figured there wasn't much left for me around Hull and was so happy to be awarded a place. I left with a lot of hope and looking to face new adventures.

• • • •

ALTHOUGH I DIDN'T REALLY know what to expect I was hoping in my heart of hearts for an exciting time and to meet new people and friends. But it didn't turn out that way. What I got instead was being alone for two years and self-isolating again. The usual pattern followed of hiding from people, not going to lessons and generally living the loneliest two years of my life, all because of OCD.

• • • •

I TRIED, I REALLY DID, and at first pushed myself, even going out a few times with the guys from the course. But slowly, OCD got the better of me and I'd take off into the confines of my room in the student halls. I could hear others on the floor through the walls talking about me and wondering if I was ok. They would sometimes knock on the door but I pretended not to be in. Sitting there in silence; with no noise, tv, or music I'd be willing them to leave me alone. All the while I'd be looking at my skin and at my hair which was starting to thin.

• • • •

I WANTED SO MUCH TO be happy and have friends but instead I had been banished to obsession hell. Days were spent in silence in my room not wanting to attract any attention, I'd sit and read books or draw instead. I ended up becoming quite the reader, finishing off most of Dickens and a bunch of other classic novels.

• • • •

THERE WAS NO TOILET in the room so I'd even go the lengths of urinating in a bottle to avoid leaving. I'd wait and sneak out late at night when the coast was clear and empty the contents down the toilet. The things I'd do to avoid looks from others.

• • • •

I TOOK TO LEAVING EARLY in the morning at around eight o'clock and making sure to stay out all day until late at night. That time was spent in parks on my own or walking around with no real aim or purpose. I'd seek out new places to sit or different routes to walk but always solo. Always wondering what people thought about my skin and hair. I'd regularly take my mirror out and look in it, seeking some kind of reassurance that no amount of checking would get me. I persisted with this, even in the deepest, darkest winter, sat alone in freezing weather in the park with just the mirror for company feeling so desperate, sad and totally alone. The obsession clinging to me tightly, not letting go for one second.

• • • •

**Do you find you isolate yourself from others, If so, why?
Can you pinpoint the reason?**

• • • •

I WOULD TRAVEL BACK home every other weekend to visit family but for those two weeks at university I'd probably speak less than a dozen times as I had nobody to talk to. Looking back, it's amazing the cages we build around ourselves without realising it. I had created my own circle of hell and all because of OCD. I would eat McDonalds everyday as I couldn't go into the student kitchen in case I was seen, I would sit in these McDonalds looking at the people sat together laughing and enjoying each other's company, I would listen in to their conversations and sometimes smile at their stories, I was living vicariously through strangers' life's as I had none of my own. A sad place for a 19-year-old to be in and also a mentally dangerous place.

• • • •

LOOKING BACK NOW I was in alot of danger during those years, I lost my grandad while I was going through all of this and that rocked my world to the core. Problem was I was good at hiding this distress from my family when I went home. I am lucky to have come through that experience as it easily could have led to mental breakdowns or even suicide.

• • • •

**Are you in your early 20's facing this type of isolation?
Do you feel alone all the time?**

• • • •

IF SO, I WOULD URGE you to talk, even to your mum or dad, or see your doctor as often talking to a stranger can be easier than talking to a loved one.

• • • •

AS MY TIME AT UNIVERSITY moved on I tried again to push myself out of my self-made trap. On one occasion I went out with a few class colleagues trying to spur myself on to make friends and embrace the *fun* university life that was all around and which had so far eluded me. As always, I remember slipping the mirror into my pocket just before heading out. We all crammed into a bar and, waiting to get served I couldn't help but pull the mirror out of my pocket just for one quick *check*, for that constant bit of reassurance I needed. To my dismay, one of the guys from the course spotted the mirror and incredulously remarked,

. . . .

*"I CAN'T BELIEVE YOU'RE looking at yourself in a mirror. At a BAR!
You are so vain, I've never seen anything like it before!'*

. . . .

I LAUGHED WEAKLY AND tried to shrug it off with a measly, *"Yer"*
but inside felt devastated. Matters were made worse when he couldn't
resist telling others. He was right about what he'd seen but his judgement
had been so far wide of the mark, it was enough to crush any last embers
of confidence in me. This was pretty much the last time I went out at
university. I was just too mortified and embarrassed, so decided that
being alone was better than feeling like sh@t. It seemed to be the lesser
of two evils.

. . . .

PEOPLE OFTEN PREY ON others weaknesses, and once found they
have this self-important persona, like they have something over you.
Often these types of people will gleefully tell others what they saw or
heard about you in complete and utter ignorance of the devastating
effect this would have on you. It's like your power is taken away in these
situations, you feel helpless as others gloat about your sad actions.

. . . .

**Have others gossiped about your distressing actions?
Can you take back the power by confronting them?
Can you show them and others your inner strength?**

. . . .

TRY IT, IT MAY BE SCARY but often people back down and look
foolish to others when the truth is brought out. A mental illness is not
for gossip, and you would be surprised by the amount of people that

actually do have mental health issues be it anxiety, depression and even OCD.

• • • •

ANOTHER MEMORY THAT highlights just how alone I was at this point in my life was being out on one of many long walks in the town centre near the university. It was a Sunday and as I walked past rows of shops, I noticed a pub with a large window in the front. Walking by I glanced in and saw four people from my course all sitting together laughing and enjoying a beer. I couldn't help but stop a moment to watch them enjoying themselves, they seemed so happy. Rather than going in and saying hi, I just carried on by, walking the usual lonely pilgrimage but now with an even slightly darker and sadder cloud hanging over me.

• • • •

I AM NOT WRITING THIS for sympathy but to show the extent a mental disorder can drive you. How far it can push at your seams and the darkness it's able to invoke. I must have seemed odd to these people off the course, this guy who never really spoke and would disappear as soon as the class finished.

• • • •

Do you know someone who acts like this?
University can be a very lonely place for some people, could you help them?

• • • •

TALKING TO A PERSON like this can be the highlight of their day, to be acknowledged and to have someone interested in you can boost the person's confidence. So, talk to them and make their day!

• • • •

OCD IS ILLUSORY. IT tricks you into thinking you have some control over what you are doing. That checking your skin or counting steps will protect you or somehow keep the bad stuff away. Like those actions will neutralise it all but that's not true. All it does is ensnare the sufferer in a cycle of going round and around without stopping, with no way to climb off. The key to living and overcoming OCD is to break these cycles. You need to find the weakest link to finally be free.

I've often looked at myself and realised that like any addiction, you must admit there is a problem before you can take the first steps to help yourself. Just like alcoholism if you can't admit there's an issue then how on earth are you going to help yourself? My obsession with appearance was triggered by the onset of teenage acne and then again when my hair started to thin. Both of these situations fuelled the fire of OCD and intrusive thoughts. At the time I didn't think spending five hours washing my hair was at all odd (yes, I did actually do this once) or carrying a mirror around to look at constantly was strange and so it was hard to see that I had such a big problem.

· · · ·

LIKE A DRUG ADDICT I slowly weaned myself off looking in the mirror and as far as the hair went, well in the end I shaved it all off! Shaving my hair short did help as I had no hair wash now! I still felt sad but also a little stronger by facing the problem. I guess what I'm saying here is that there is always a way through these things even If they seem hard. There is always a path through for you.

· · · ·

I SAW UNIVERSITY OUT to the bitter end. Despite it being hard and lonely I gained a few things from that time; resilience and knowing that I could be ok in my own company. Almost like a superpower, the ability to be ok alone with my own thoughts.

Once the course finished I decided to go travelling. It was a chance to clear my head and hopefully find a little peace with all the appearance stuff and myself overall. I was still sad a lot of the time and felt alone but there was only a single way forward, to put one foot in front of the other and walk on.

• • • •

Can you take that first step forward?
Can you take that scary leap to start fighting back against OCD?
You have this book now, so in a way you have taken your first step. You know you're not alone. Well done!

The American Dream

I needed some much-needed time and recovery after the university 'experience', so I decided to apply and work in America in one of their summer camps. Thankfully, my application was accepted and upon passing the interview stage, off to the land of opportunity I trotted, yeehaw!

$\bullet\ \bullet\ \bullet\ \bullet$

FIRST STOP WAS A PLACE called Raquette Lake near the border of Canada and what an *amazing* place this was! Mountains and lakes as far as the eye could see with thousands of miles of beautiful, untouched country to enjoy for the next two months. Despite feeling a bit scared I jumped right into camp life.

$\bullet\ \bullet\ \bullet\ \bullet$

STILL SHAKEN FROM A bad university time and the relationship with Zoe, it was hard to fight the instinct not to hide away at camp but as the days passed I grew in confidence. My skin began to clear up in the warm sunny climate, helping me to feel better and rely less and less on the mirror. Things improved further still when I made some friends and started to feel happier. Finally, there seemed to be a way forward for me.

$\bullet\ \bullet\ \bullet\ \bullet$

WHEN CAMP ENDED I WANTED to see more of America so travelled around for a month, once again pushing through feelings of fear to pursue an exciting experience. Even though I would still look in the mirror more than I should, it didn't stop me being positive and enjoying the experience.

$\bullet\ \bullet\ \bullet\ \bullet$

I RETURNED TO THE UK with a much more positive outlook, travelling had been one of the best experiences, like I'd almost been able to reinvent myself whilst away. I had a newfound confidence that meant I felt ready to take another shot at university.

. . . .

BY PUSHING MYSELF THESE positive experiences helped to regain some of my much-lost confidence. It was difficult to start with and yes, I did struggle at times but pushing myself like this helped me step out of the shadow of OCD, if only for a few moments in time.

*Maybe
you don't have to push yourself forward.
Maybe you just have to*
STOP HOLDING YOURSELF BACK
Authur - Doe Zantamata

Yes, you are reading correctly... unbelievably I went to university for a **SECOND TIME**.

• • • •

I DECIDED TO TRY LIVING the university dream again to somehow repair the damage from the first time around. I still had hang ups about my looks and still carried the mirror like a crux but had less urgency to use it now feeling more secure than before. This was a *big* step, the first university experience had left me alone and disillusioned but working and living in America had offered me some hope. Going back to university again felt like a real gamble but I just couldn't accept the first negative experience I'd been dealt. I needed to clean the slate and start over.

For the first year my second take at university turned out to be *amazing*! I met some of the best people and made lifelong friends. It was the university life I had hoped for and more. I was in a stronger position this time being a few years older than the rest of them. I'd also been off travelling which had given me life experience that most people didn't have at that stage in their lives.

• • • •

I MET FRIENDS FROM day one, we hung out together and got very drunk on many occasions. They didn't judge or put me down in any way. Yes, I still had my issues, but I was accepted... finally!

• • • •

HOWEVER, NEAR THE END of the degree when I was about twenty-five years old, the negative thoughts started to creep back in.

I properly began to lose my hair and would spend hours washing and combing it just trying to make it look ok.

· · · ·

GOD, LOOKING BACK IT was so easy to slip back into this obsession with the way I looked, only now my hair had replaced my skin. This was my new OCD trigger and it was all tied into my appearance again.

· · · ·

AS A SENSITIVE INDIVIDUAL, I was very susceptible to feeling negative about how I looked. The teenage years had shown this and now my hair was really affecting me, dragging all these negative feelings back. I felt sad inside, I was only twenty five and my hair was thinning and receding. What a blow to my self-confidence which had thrown open the door to that unwelcome visitor OCD yet again.

· · · ·

IMAGINE HATING THE way you look, avoiding mirrors and even reflections in windows, well this was how I felt, how I always felt inside now I think about it. Spending hours looking in the mirror, making me drained, exhausted, and unable to stop until satisfied I was acceptable to others. That's right, being acceptable to **'Others'** is what drove me in my madness, having others accept me made me feel better about myself. Another form of a trap.

· · · ·

I KNEW, DEEP DOWN, that a lot of this was *not* how I appeared to people but I was my own harshest critic, constantly berating my reflection in the mirror with '*You can't go out if you don't look ok.*' And so for yet a second time, I was 'trapped in the cycle.' My OCD was about self-image and how I looked outwardly, and it drove me to going to extreme lengths to try and make myself feel ok, literally hours of life wasted.

• • • •

Have you been trapped like this?
Going to extreme lengths?
Doing whatever it takes to feel ok about yourself?

• • • •

YOU NEED TO ACKNOWLEDGE that you are, as it is the only way to move forward and help yourself. Remember, only you can do this but help is out there for you.

• • • •

DURING MY TIME AT UNIVERSITY I worked, I really couldn't afford not to so took on a bar job again as it was something I knew my way around. In hindsight (that wonderful thing) this was a possible mistake as it put me in the firing line of hundreds of people each week, talk about walking into the lion's den.

• • • •

THIS TIME I WAS AT the bar serving drinks to people, a job I enjoyed *but* my hair was starting to thin, so I'd go to more extreme lengths to hide the fact I was losing it. I'd try to tackle the problem by growing the back longer and combing it forward, then combine it all with a ton of hair spray to hold everything in place. I'd even check the weather in advance to make sure it wasn't windy or going to rain as those conditions would have an adverse effect on my hair, making the hairspray run away so that people would be able to see it's thinness.

• • • •

THIS CHECKING AGAIN of the weather made me unhappy, I kept on asking myself "how long had I spent 'checking things' and how long could I go on like this?"

. . . .

I'D BEEN BEHIND THE bar for two years at uni and in that time I had seen people pointing at me and talking which I tried to ignore as best I could but things came to a head one evening. It was a Saturday night; and as usual, the bar was rammed three people deep. I was at the front taking orders, whilst a group of men stood in front of me and began to laugh as they pointed mockingly at my hair. The laughter got harder as they jeered about how ridiculous it looked. I had nowhere to hide, like a deer caught in the headlights. I felt tiny and totally destroyed by this act and it wasn't just them looking at me either, by this point their shouting had drawn attention from half of the bar who were now all staring at my hair and how bad it was. I'm a big man but had never felt as small as I did that evening.

. . . .

A BAR FULL OF EYES watching, judging, laughing at me. I wanted to bolt and hide, I was sweating heavily from the shame I felt which of course made things look even worse with my hair.

. . . .

AS THE POINTING AND laughing faded, these people got their drinks and left the bar area. I next served a woman who had seen it all and she said quietly, 'I think you look great, don't listen to them.' This nearly made me cry right there at the bar in front of maybe a hundred people. I replied 'thank you' then shuffled off the bar to breath and regroup in the backroom.

. . . .

IT WAS HEARTENING TO find there was also kindness out there. I left the job later that week, I just couldn't put myself in front of people again. I did really like the work, I liked the people I worked with and even most of the local customers. I felt heavy leaving it but could not face being a spectacle to people.

Have you ever stopped doing something because of your OCD? Has OCD affected you in a way that meant you couldn't enjoy life?

• • • •

A MENTAL ILLNESS CAN prevent you from starting something new or even stop you doing what you love. It has the power to strip away those things and take whole sections of your life. It's isolating and can make you withdraw into a box, a box you think you can control, but it's empty with just you in it. There's a famous saying.

'Think Outside the Box'

• • • •

WELL, MY PERSONAL SAYING is

'Live Outside the Box'

Don't be fooled into thinking being alone is best.

• • • •

AFTER LEAVING THE BAR, I worked in a hotel as a night porter, which suited me as it meant I was alone all night in the hotel. I hid away in the job and started sleeping during the day and working at night. I almost became a hermit during that time.

• • • •

MY HAIR WAS REALLY starting to affect me in an extremely negative way. I just couldn't stop focusing on it and how I looked to others, which led to a very distressing event that lasted a full day. I call this day,

The university course had just finished and all my uni friends had gone home. I was now living alone in my student flat and was going to work for a few months before heading home myself.

• • • •

THE DAY STARTED AS normal, I got up early with a plan to pop out to the shops for food and drink as I'd started drinking alcohol quite heavily at this point in my life. I would regularly drink three to four bottles of wine every other day topped up with large bottles of cider and vodka, as a way of forgetting.

• • • •

FIRST THING I DID WAKING up was to look in the mirror and I saw that my hair was a complete mess. It was matted and stiff from all the hairspray I was using and needed resetting again. I had to go through my usual ritual of washing it and trying to make it look ok. I washed and dried it, doing so by using a towel and rubbing from back to front only, trying obsessively to get my thinning hairs to lay down neatly, followed with a load of hairspray, spraying from back to front and using a comb to gently tease the hairs into line. It didn't look good at all after my first attempt. To my troubled eyes, the end result was totally wrong so I had to start washing it all over again.

• • • •

THE VOICE IN MY HEAD was saying,

• • • •

'You look stupid, you can't go out like this as people will look at you and laugh, you need to fix it'

. . . .

I WAS CAUGHT IN A RINSE and repeat cycle that ended up lasting around nine hours. Washing my hair, using the hair spray, looking at myself, feeling bad at how I looked. Starting again, washing my hair, using the hair spray, looking at myself. Every time it looked bad so I would press the start button on the cycle again.

. . . .

BY THE END OF THIS I was utterly exhausted, wrung out. I had no energy left to leave the house so I just gave up and didn't eat. It seemed easier than starting over with my hair.

. . . .

I LOST NINE HOURS TO OCD, I didn't leave the house or even eat until the next day. During those nine hours I could feel myself getting increasingly panicked, I couldn't leave the cycle. I couldn't leave the flat. I *had* to keep going until my OCD mind was satisfied, until I was spent and the OCD was finally satisfied. It was a day of hell.

. . . .

IT WAS 'The Day I Lost'

. . . .

ON A SECOND OCCASSION I was due to go out with my uni mates. In preparation I'd brushed and used lots of hair spray to keep my hair still but this alone made it look odd so I'd combed the back forward (which I'd grown longer.) Not a great look at all but I was obsessed and desperate again.

. . . .

WHILST WE WERE IN THE city centre another group started pointing and ridiculing my hair, saying *'wonder where his hairline starts'* then laughing even harder, which made me feel like sh@t. After years and years of self torture, I finally felt better about my skin only for my hair to become the new obsession. Being pointed at and laughed in public is the ultimate humiliation. Again, I was picked on by a group of people who caredless for what I was going through.

• • • •

PEOPLE CAN BE SO CRUEL, mocking others and not caring about the effect they are having on them or what damage they are doing to that person.

Writing this, I am fully opening up my mind and the events that have made me who I am today to give an insight into what OCD can do. Ultimately I'm hoping it shows you are not alone in living with it or living with someone who has OCD. Remember there is a way through this,

• • • •

*YOU **CAN** take back control of your life.*
*You **CAN** be your best self without listening to that voice in your head.*
*You **CAN** be strong.*

Even to this day now, as a forty two year old man I can get caught up in this cycle a little. I sometimes look at myself then head back to the mirror and look again, then a third time. The difference now is that I can break the cycle and walk away instead of getting caught up for hours and hours in an exhausting obsession that leaves you mentally and physically drained. I broke the chain and so can you!

• • • •

NOW THAT I'M OLDER I feel like a veteran of this OCD, I feel it in my mind at times trying to control me, trying to distract me. Yes, sometimes it does distract me but being aware of it I can distract myself and turn my mind to other things much easier than I could as a young man.

My younger years were exhausting with some good times but lots of acting at being happy or confident when inside all my senses were screaming at me,

• • • •

'what do I look like'
    ' why are they looking at me'

      'I need to leave here and be on my own'
      'I can't carry on'.

'I can't carry on', what a scary thought, to be at a point where a mental health condition has pushed you to such a sad and desperate conclusion. Millions of people every second of every day have this thought and see this as a final way out of a cycle of desperation that a mental disorder like OCD can push you into.

Recent "The Lockdown" Years

A good fifteen years has passed since I started this book (yep, I like to take my sweet time 😊) and I've had ups and downs regarding my own issues with OCD. I still have hang ups with my appearance and still sometimes get *"trapped in the cycle"*, of having to check in a mirror to make sure I look ok. I also have the odd doubt about who I am and feel moments of my strength wavering but I try to take a deep breath and tell myself, *"Lee, you're doing ok and you can do it."*

· · · ·

IN RECENT YEARS LIFE has taken some crazy and difficult turns. I separated from my partner who I have two kids with and then COVID-19 kicked in. The lockdowns were, I'm sure you'd agree, a period in which many people's mental health was put to the test. During this time, my ex partner who also had OCD really suffered and the thought of getting this virus pushed her into new lows of anxiety and stress as she refused to leave the marital home with the kids for fear of covid. It involved me having to buy food and take it to the house but leave it in the garage so she could sanitise everything. All the while she'd refuse to open the door in case it let the *'virus'* in and refuse to talk to me because she didn't think I'd washed my hands properly.

· · · ·

TURNS OUT THERE WAS a second virus during the pandemic and it was the spread of mental health issues. OCD flared up like a wildfire, raging through people that were locked away behind closed doors and making them even more fearful of venturing out when they were allowed. Its impact I fear, will last for years especially in those who already suffered from OCD and other mental health conditions, as it has just exacerbated them.

Mental health problems have been on the rise massively since those first days of corona.

• • • •

'Statistically significant increase in OCD severity in all OCD dimensions during the COVID-19 pandemic compared with pre-pandemic levels'.
SOURCE NATIONAL INSTITUTE of Health

• • • •

PROBLEMS THAT WOULD have only been a small issue have magnified tenfold, especially in people that already struggled with things being dirty.

• • • •

YOU SEE, ANOTHER FORM of OCD can also show up as needing to clean your hands or body and even objects to remove '*germs*'. Imagine someone who was stressed and was obsessed with this in their everyday life before COVID and then BOOM, suddenly COVID set in, now there's a whole world of lockdown fuelling this mental disease!

• • • •

YES, THE AVERAGE PERSON did clean their hands more as per the government's guidelines during this period but imagine what the OCD sufferer was like, and the extent to which they cleaned their hands and body and home. A new phenomenon that emerged that focused on a person and them literally bleach spraying their packaged food to '*decontaminate*' it.

• • • •

I WENT THROUGH ALL this with my ex partner who would fervently spray and wash any packaged foods that came near her home. They were all sprayed down with anti bacterial sprays and left for days in the garage until deemed safe enough to use.

• • • •

I ONCE BROUGHT HER some groceries and walked in the back door without sanitising my shoes or the food in the bag. I just didn't think and, well, she went insane, telling me I was infecting them all and didn't care and couldn't do anything right. I felt like sh@t and was made to stand out in the back garden, only being allowed back in if I washed my hands in a bowl of bleach and sprayed my clothes down with the bleach spray. I felt humiliated and sad at having to do such a thing, like a dog being told off but she was in the grip of her OCD fever which had significantly increased with the covid lockdown and fed into this cycle of OCD madness. I felt I had no choice but to go along with it and try to alleviate her stress levels. It wasn't her doing this or me, it was OCD controlling the situation.

• • • •

SHE USED TO WASH HER hands until they actually bled. Until they were red raw and dry with peeling skin but she couldn't stop it. To her it was the only way to prevent the virus even though she never left the house.

• • • •

SUCH IRRATIONAL ACTION all makes sense to the OCD sufferer who's "trapped in the cycle". So remember, now you've had a feeling of what it's like to be more obsessed with cleaning yourself from measures set out in the pandemic, imagine the impact this has had on a person who already suffers from OCD.

• • • •

MY QUESTION IS THIS, I wonder how many more people have developed OCD during the lockdowns? And what has been the mental health impact on society, including our children?

• • • •

FOR MY CHILDREN I HAVE noticed a change in my son since the pandemic, a need to clean his hands often and an aversion to even touching food that someone else has touched. He's now 8 and I'm trying to help him with this by talking to him about it. I've since had a breakthrough and he drank from a water bottle of mine!

• • • •

I NOTICED AN ODD REACTION to myself during the pandemic, being 6ft 3inches and an unusually big in stature person, I seemed to stand out even more. People would look at me like I was a threat, almost like I was the virus. The government's two metre rule highlighted people's aversion to being near me. They would actively move away and avoid me and this did start to make me more aware of myself again and become more self conscious but I stopped myself falling back into the cycle as I vowed never to go back to that.

• • • •

I REMEMBER ONE OCCASION i was standing within 2 metres of the lady in front and she turned around looking at me like i was a monster and shouted 'get back away from me'. What a shock to me and the incident gave me flashbacks to the days when I hid away. Still, people were gripped in a madness at the time

Well lockdown came and went and the pandemic never left, but new levels of mental health have dramatically risen during these years, keeping clean, always washing your hands, not going near people, avoiding contact with others, not wanting to touch surfaces, freaking out if someone coughs near you.

•••••

THESE ALL SOUND LIKE symptoms of a person who has a mental health issue like OCD, this is the reality we all lived in and still do.

•••••

THESE ACTIVITIES HAVE become compulsions in many many people now, do you worry about touching a surface? Or if someone comes too close to you? If you answer yes then maybe you're getting "trapped in the cycle" and the very government advice is becoming an obsession to you.

There are no miracle cures, you're not going to change overnight, but you can step by step learn to control it.

• • • •

THE FACT IS MOST PEOPLE have OCD to some small degree, how many times do you check your keys in your pocket? How many times do you make sure you have your railcards in your coat even though you know they're there? How many times does a person check their change even though they've counted it two or three times? everyone does that's the answer.

• • • •

SO EVERYONE HAS IT to a small degree but some people like me and people I know let it be their life, it stops being a little annoyance and ends up being your master and ruler, does this sound familiar?

• • • •

A PERSON WHO DOESN'T really suffer from OCD can easily walk through a door or wash their hands once, a person who does suffer from OCD might have to walk through the door over and over again, they might have to wash their hands dozens and dozens of times and still feel dirty. This repetitive task is why it's called Obsessive Compulsive Disorder, it's a repetitive task done over and over again to the point of distress.

• • • •

THERE IS ONE REALLY distressing form of OCD that people will probably never tell anyone about. I have known someone who suffered from it and it's extremely distressing for them and I feel it needs to be mentioned, this form is called '*Cancelling Out*' or '*Unwanted Sexual Thoughts*'.

• • • •

THE SUFFERER HAS IMAGES in their head that they've hurt a child or they have fears that there paedophile's, an extremely distressing thought as you can imagine. My experience of this is of a friend, she had these distressing thoughts and images in her head for no reason what's so ever and she only ever told me about it, I told her these thoughts and images don't make you evil or a paedophile at all!!! It's just your mind playing tricks on you.

Even though I reassured her over and over again she found it hard to accept this and had doubts about herself, I kept on and told her these images mean nothing, they will pass, so please don't distress yourself if this has happened to you, you're not alone.

• • • •

THESE IMAGES WILL PASS, you need to let them go and not to hold onto them, having any distressing image in your mind is hard, it makes you worry and think '*why am I thinking these thoughts? And I must be bad if that's in my mind!*'.

• • • •

MENTAL IMAGES COME and go all the time and like air they have no substance and will fade and disappear, try not to hold onto an image in your mind that's disturbing you, easier said than done I know as I've had distressing thoughts myself. I think for me it was to focus on something that's positive in my life like an event or a person and the bad image gradually fades away.

Don't worry if the image comes back as the mind has a way of recycling bad things but try and let the image go. Let it appear but don't give it any power, don't focus on it and let it drift away while allowing other much better and happier thoughts enter your mind.

• • • •

OUR BRAINS ARE COMPLICATED machines and we only know a fraction of how our brain works and what we actually are.

• • • •

What is consciousness?
What are you?
Who are you?

• • • •

ALL DEEP QUESTIONS that no scientist really knows so don't beat yourself up if you struggle from time to time with bad thoughts or images.

• • • •

ANOTHER PERSON I KNEW would cut out articles and images out of newspapers, she would buy up to 10 newspapers a day and spend each evening cutting articles and images out and placing them in plastic folders. She never went back to these articles or images but horded them in masses of files. This is a different form of OCD, collecting things for no reason, hoarding and obsessing over items that actually adds no value to your life.

• • • •

YOU MAY HAVE SEEN THIS in its extreme form on TV, this is people who have houses literally full of stuff they have collected over the years, to the point we're there's no room to move in their houses. There's TV programmes dedicated to these 'collectors' of things, a person with this type of OCD often puts a false value on the objects to the point when they can't let go of them.

• • • •

SOME PEOPLE LIVE MOST of their life living like this, in a house full of collected items and not able to let go of even a single thing. How hard it must be living like this trapped in a tomb of collected items.

There are many other forms of OCD but let's face it, you don't really need to know right, and if you do I have provided links at the end to assist you. My real reason is to try and help you not scare you more, so let's continue and look at what it's like living with someone who has OCD, how you have to live in there world and the difficulties it creates, a subject that's all too often overlooked I think.

Non OCD Sufferer Point of View

Most articles and forums are for people who suffer from OCD but I think it's just as distressing to be the one who lives with the person with OCD.

With this in mind I've taken this chapter to write about it and explain why it's really difficult for the non-sufferer. I'm going to try and explain it from my own past and point of view as I think this will be more real and informative then just explaining why it's hard.

• • • •

I'LL START BY TELLING my story of living with someone with OCD but please remember, I'm explaining it in the way I felt at the time and now I know the person didn't mean anything she said to me.

• • • •

MY FIRST EXPERIENCE of being around someone else with OCD started when I met **Zoe.** I talked about Zoe early in this book but now I feel I can go into more detail about living with someone who has OCD and the huge struggles that come along with that.

• • • •

I MET **Zoe** on a night out through a friend as I talked about at the beginning of the book. She was great, and I fell for her instantly. A week into seeing her I noticed when I was at her house she used to disappear a lot and not really explain why, I didn't really think anything of it to be honest, but this came to a crunch a few days later when she told me she had a problem and that she didn't really want to tell me because I treated her so normal, which it seemed was something she was not used too.

• • • •

SHE WENT ON TO TELL me that she has something called OCD, at the time I had no idea what it really was but as she explained I realised that I had also suffered from it in my teens in my own way, I told her not to worry and we just carried on.

· · · ·

ZOE and I fell for each other, Zoe lived in her own house so it meant I could stay there whenever I wanted, this ended up being five or six days out of seven.

I started to notice things start to change when I was at her house as the first thing she started to say to me was to wash my hands, not once not twice but at least three times at a time, sometimes four or five times a day. This was as I entered the door, I always did this, she'd make me shower, wash my hair, even change my clothes. At this point I was starting to get distressed myself and couldn't truly understand what was happening to this fun girl I met months ago but I loved her, what could I do?

· · · ·

AS TIME WENT ON THINGS got worse and worse, she'd scream at me if I didn't do something correctly such as feed her cat or put pots in the dishwasher machine right, every action I made I had to think ahead planning my actions because I knew if I did something slightly wrong she would go crazy at me, but I knew it wasn't really her talking.

· · · ·

I KNEW THIS AND THIS kept me going, I told myself I'm not the sort of person to quit!!

· · · ·

THIS ALL GOT TO A HEAD when I organised a trip for her birthday, this involved going horse riding and to a restaurant. I planned everything and even got my mum to drive us. My mistake was turning up to her house 20 minutes early, I walked in and instantly she started shouting and screaming at me saying *you've ruined my day, why do you always do this, I hate you*, as you can imagine this made me feel like s**t, real bad, and for the rest of the day she hardly spoke to me or even smiled. This made me feel angry, sad and embarrassed as the whole event was witnessed by my family. I thought to myself *How could she do this to me, what have I done to deserve this?*

• • • •

AT TIMES SHE USED TO be a heap on the floor crying her eyes out with me sitting there feeling so stressed not knowing what to say or do to help her. I thought I could somehow miraculously cure her and everything would be ok but let's face it reader this only really happens in the movies.

• • • •

I MYSELF USED TO BREAK down in tears. I'll admit it, I was under so much stress and my health suffered, I lost weight, I stopped sleeping, I felt ill all the time and I was a real mess.

The problem was I loved her and I didn't want to leave her but I felt at the time that she was growing to resent me as I appeared to cause a lot of her problems and disturbed her routine life. Looking back I realise that she would have these problems even if I wasn't there. (**OCD is isolating, like alcoholism**)

• • • •

WE DID BREAK UP IN the end, I was young and had no real understanding of what she was suffering from and at the time I was getting angry towards her thinking *Why did she treat me this way, Why was she always shouting at me*.

• • • •

I LOST WEIGHT AT THE end and was a shadow of my true self. I dug in with her and tried my best to help her and be with her, but sometimes you just run out of fight and you then have to look at yourself and your own health and wellbeing. I sacrificed a lot looking back and nearly lost myself in the process of trying to help her, just remember if you fall, who's going to lift you up?

• • • •

NOW WITH TIME AND A little wisdom I realise the issues she was going through and know she didn't mean anything she said but you must understand that at the time I guess I was trying my best. I did only what I knew at the time, and now I put to you that people who live with others who have OCD suffer greatly as well!.

You need to realise that the person living with you isn't you and doesn't have the same thoughts as you. It wouldn't occur to your loved one to wash their hands three or four times or to obsessively straighten objects in your home.

• • • •

IT'S HARD TO LIVE IN someone else's world, especially one who suffers from OCD. Your loved one cares for you and would do anything for you but don't punish them if they do something that distresses you. To you the action might be disturbing and wrong but to your loved one it would seem normal, everyday, an action everybody does. Please remember they are trying to live in **your** world and it's not easy.

• • • •

I RECENTLY GOT AN EMAIL from a young man and it sounded like he was in the same position I was, he said that his girlfriend suffered greatly from OCD and she screamed and self hurt and he was in tears every day. It made me really sad to read it as I know he loves her and would do anything for her. I gave him some advice from experience and I hope it helped.

. . . .

THIS LETTER MADE ME realise more than ever that there's two people in the relationship and this point of view from the loved one or friend has to be made aware of.

. . . .

WE CAN GET ANGRY WITH a person who suffers from OCD, they're doing something over and over again and if you don't have OCD you just don't get it. You don't get the repetitive task or the constant counting or cleaning, it just doesn't make sense and can lead to resentment. I've felt this way about loved ones I've lived with but now looking back I'm not getting angry at them I'm getting angry at the helplessness of the situation and that I can't help them or really know how to stop their suffering.

. . . .

LET'S FACE IT YOU WOULD walk over hot coals for your loved ones and this helplessness you may be feeling makes you feel angry, you will snap at your loved one and get angry but please step back and realise it's the situation you're angry at not the person. Their actions may not make sense to you but being angry and shouting at them will compound the situation, calm is needed here reader, and understanding as best you can.

With the recent pandemic obsessive compulsive disorders have become much more common in adults but an area sometimes overlooked is our children. It's much harder to spot an obsessive compulsive disorder in a child as they often don't really know what they're doing and can often mask the disorder or it can simply be looked at as play.

. . . .

I NOTICED A BIT OF this with my own children, as the pandemic dug in so did the need for my kids to wash their hands, their mother suffered badly from OCD as I've already mentioned and I believe this passed onto my kids in a way. I'd be out with them and they would insist on washing their hands all the time and they didn't want to touch surfaces in case 'the virus' got them, as my son would say.

. . . .

I ALSO NOTICED THEM spotting things on the ground and insisting on going back to check on it, this is also a thing their mother had. She would often stop and go back to check on something on the floor saying to me, 'I need to check that out just in case'. Not having the type of OCD she had I found it odd and sometimes frustrating having to stop all the time, I had to live in her world and it often didn't make sense to me, this is true understanding comes in.

. . . .

TALK WITH YOUR CHILD if you see anything that could be classed as OCD, ask them 'I see you're putting things straight a lot, is that to make yourself feel better?' this may open them up a little and they may talk to you, as I said they might not even realise they're doing anything.

• • • •

AGAIN WITH CHILDREN the sooner any of these issues are noticed the better for the kids and the easier it is to deal with and talk to them about it. This ongoing pandemic created kids and adults who are falling into the OCD cycle trap.

• • • •

PLEASE DON'T BE ONE of them!

The OCD Sufferer Point of View

I myself suffered from a form of OCD during my teens going through to university and just after, everything I did made complete sense to me at the time and was something I had to do, it was a compulsion as strong as breathing air.

. . . .

I WAS ONCE OUT WITH my friends and as I previously said I had very real issues with my appearance off the back of years of acne and hiding away from people, I again had this mirror in my pocket which I used to look at myself with.

. . . .

ON THIS NIGHT I WENT into the toilets and went into a cubicle and got the mirror out to use it. As I did this a bouncer looked over the cubicle and saw me, obviously I reacted and put it back in my pocket. He asked *what was I doing*, and I said nothing and I left the toilets.

. . . .

MY COMPULSION TO LOOK at myself came again a while later so I went back into the toilet cubicle to get the mirror out, the same bouncer must have followed me back and looked over the cubicle at me again. This time he said he was *throwing me out of the bar*, I was so embarrassed and the idea of telling my friends I was being thrown out for looking at myself with a mirror almost broke me.

. . . .

IN THE END I HAD TO stand there with the bouncer and explain like a child I had something called OCD and that it was a compulsion to look at myself in the mirror, not sure if he knew what I was talking about but he let me stay in the bar and left me alone.

• • • •

THIS WAS ONE OF THE worst times of my life and made me take a step back and look at what I was doing.

• • • •

THIS STORY MIGHT RING home to plenty of you, your OCD makes you do things over and over again and like myself looking in the mirror. Your actions almost become normal to you but to an observer its strange and odd behaviour and this can make you stand out and also make you isolated from friends, family or work.

How OCD is Trivialised in Modern Conversation

It seems the modern world has almost trivialised OCD to an extent, often in the news or around people you hear the words 'that's a bit OCD isn't it', or 'it's like I have OCD or something '. You may find people almost don't really believe in it and believe you can simply stop counting or just wash your hands once, this can make a mockery of how serious OCD actually is, like it's nearly a quirk or something humorous that people sometimes have, as if it simply passes.

· · · ·

IF WE JUST JOKE ABOUT 'how OCD we are', we're losing the seriousness of the disorder and making a mockery of all the millions of sufferers out there. OCD is a serious mental health condition that can destroy not only the sufferer's life but also the people they live with.

How OCD can be diagnosed by a professional

OCD isn't the easiest thing to actually diagnose, as you may be so set in the 'cycle' you don't even realise that something is wrong in your actions. First step is to realise something isn't right , are you doing something over and over again till you're exhausted? Do you check things over and over again until you're exhausted ? Well these are signs and symptoms of OCD and if this applies to you then please take a breath and let's look at the next step together.

· · · ·

FIRST AND BEST STEP is to talk to your local doctor about it, they are professionals but maybe not with OCD so you would be referred to a specialist who will talk to you and dig a bit deeper into where this has come from. There is often a starting Point to OCD, for me it was a lack of confidence in my appearance with acne that started my issues and this flared and burned out of control into my teens and into young adulthood. For you it may be different but a professional can really help.

· · · ·

MY EX PARTNER WENT to a professional for help and I accompanied her to the sessions. She was nervous and let's face it, you're letting yourself out and baring your soul to a stranger but it really did help her and helped her to see the destructive cycle she was in. This professional also gave her ways of handling situations that would have freaked her out and made her trapped for hours going over and over the same problem, this is ongoing holistic help.

· · · ·

TALKING TO A CLOSE friend or partner about how your feeling can also really help, they can see things from different perspectives from yourself and can often give advice or help, but if this is too personal then talking to a stranger is often much easier.

• • • •

PLEASE DON'T BE TRAPPED and give help a chance, ◈ sometimes you have to let go

Someone who suffers from OCD might not admit it and might avoid it but they need a helping hand, this can be simply understanding what they are going through and making life easier for them. It could also be going with them to therapy or giving advice.

• • • •

ONE THING I HAVE LEARNT the hard way is if you always go along with them and try to live in their world you won't be helping a sufferer and you won't be helping yourself at all, this path leads to depression and possibly even enabling further the issues the OCD sufferer has.

• • • •

NO ONE WANTS OCD OR anxiety, that's a fact, so hold on and be patient with your loved one even if what's happening makes no sense at the time.

The way through the maze of OCD starts with you, you have to help yourself and make the first steps. What you shouldn't do is numb yourself by taking drugs, antidepressants or alcohol as in my humble opinion only numbs your feelings or actions like a mask, not getting to the root of the issues.

• • • •

THERE'S A GREAT SAYING, *'From the root to the fruit!!!'* and these statements are so true. A person who has OCD has to start at the beginning, you have to start with the root and the underlying causes, starting here could be a simple action of taking a chance or talking to someone.

• • • •

KEEP A DIARY AS THIS can be used to monitor yourself, some people with OCD worry that they have done something to someone and keeping a diary of your day to day life would enable you to look back and see that it's just your mind playing tricks on you.

• • • •

COUNSELLING IS A GREAT way to help cope with OCD, there seems to be a stigma that if you go and see a therapist you're crazy or you've failed. This is completely not true as this can be one of the most effective ways of dealing with OCD, you may not want to go or a loved one may even refuse to go with you, but please consider this, go with a friend or a partner if your nervous as this can help and even bring you closer together.

• • • •

A FRIEND OF MINE SAW a councillor once a week and felt that it really helped, seeing a person who talks to you and doesn't judge may be just what you need, a person with real training at dealing with what you're going through.

. . . .

RECENTLY OCD SEEMS to have finally come into the limelight and to the media's attention which is about time, this attention can only benefit those with OCD with new treatments and more research. However, at present there is some medication that you can take but like taking alcohol this too is only a way to mask your problems, so we need to get really to the depth of the issue, a direct way to help **you** face OCD and manage it.

There is one type of therapy that I do highly recommend, this is called '**Cognitive Behaviour Therapy**', so I'm going to dedicate a whole chapter to this treatment.

Cognitive Therapy Behaviour

Cognitive Behaviour Therapy or 'CBT' means basically to '*Train your mind to think correctly*', to take control of that wild horse in your mind and tame it!!!! This is not easy at all and this isn't a miracle cure all but it will allow you to grab your life by the scruff of its neck and shout out,

· · · ·

'NOW I'M BACK IN CONTROL AND HERE TO STAY!!'.

· · · ·

CBT THERAPY CAN BE done by yourself at home or you could also go seek a good councillor trained in this technique, (at the end I will list ways of contacting such people).

· · · ·

CBT MEANS YOU FACE your fears, this could mean for some not washing their hands after they have touched something they class as dirty and for others this could mean not counting their steps as they walk. I have seen this in full effect and I can say it really can help.

· · · ·

I WENT ONCE TO SEE a counsellor with a friend of mine who suffers from OCD and this person had problems with washing their hands and a great fear of getting contaminated. The councillor we saw was also a sexual health councillor who saw and counselled people who also had Aids, yes, a big thing in any one's book.

· · · ·

HE TOLD MY FRIEND THAT he talks to and shakes the hands of those people he sees that have Aids, he then asked her to shake his hand, as you can imagine what a massive thing to ask her!!! Well she said no, so we carried on talking, he asked her what she was really scared of and told her it was her mind playing tricks on her. This went on till the end of the session and as we left he asked her again to shake his hands, reluctantly but amazingly she did, she faced her biggest fear and did it and yes she did ask me if she was going to be ok, but she did it, I told her this.

But I won't fool you reader, this wasn't a miracle breakthrough and there was a long road still to go but it was a start, she faced her fear and she had for that one moment beat OCD!!!.

• • • •

AS YOU FACE YOUR FEARS more and more the fear itself lessons, you learn to accept it and not run scared, it's all about **YOU!** taking a chance and taking the first step, yes you can have as much help as you need but only **YOU** can really help yourself! Take that first step.

• • • •

ANOTHER TECHNIQUE OF CBT especially to those who have images in their mind involves *'letting the images go'*, instead of fighting these images that appear in your mind accept their there, trust me everyone gets good, bad and scary images in their mind, I do all the time, but instead of fighting it or scaring yourself let the image appear and then pass.

• • • •

NOW THINK ABOUT IT, if I told you to imagine a red balloon in your mind you can easily do this, this is a good image. As you read on you will slowly let it pass from your mind, it just slips away, you haven't fought it, you haven't worried about it, it just goes, right? Now, no matter what image appears in your mind no matter how bad, scary or wrong you think it is, accept it's there, it doesn't make you bad or evil, accept and let It pass, don't analyse it or get worried about it, let it pass like the morning mist on a lake, let it slowly fade away.

• • • •

THIS IS ALL ABOUT TRAINING your mind, and I know it's difficult, you may hit many brick walls along the way but the more you practise the easier it gets trust me. Now let's quickly look at a way to train and focus your mind, this is called meditation.

• • • •

I'M NOT TRYING TO PUSH new age hippy stuff onto you as meditation is an ancient art of controlling one's mind and thoughts and can really help you develop good mind control, meditation is all about clearing and focusing the mind, effectively this is *non-thought*.

• • • •

THIS CAN BE DONE ALONE or with a class but the basic technique involves sitting, standing or laying down, closing your eyes and focusing on your breathing or just the silence. At first images and sound may jump into your mind, this happens, but just like I explained earlier about *'letting the image go'* that same technique applies here. Let the sound or image go and re-focus on your breathing or the silence, try to do this every day even for only five minutes. After a while you will notice it getting easier, your mind will be under more control, with a stronger more focused mind you will be more effective at controlling OCD.

This is a term I made for how I think OCD gets you *trapped in a cycle* and can be described as a 'repetitive task with almost no end to it that causes distress to the individual'

· · · ·

WE ALL HAVE THIS IN a way, checking the stove is turned off more than once or the classic checking your pockets for your keys or wallet over and over again , I do this all the time and it's not what I would call OCD, yes your checking again and again for the items but it doesn't cause you distress like OCD would. OCD would be affecting your mental well-being and the cycle almost spirals down, getting worse and worse causing more stress and anxiety.

· · · ·

BEING 'TRAPPED IN THE cycle' can consume a person both mentally and physically causing the sufferer to do physical activities over and over again. Washing their hands or checking the doors locked for hours and mentally draining activities such as counting or distressing images, this 'cycle' can often steal large parts of your day away as it did with me looking at myself, I lost hrs upon hrs of my day when I had it at its worse.

· · · ·

WHAT A WASTE OF YOUR time and life all the hours and days lost being 'trapped' like this doing a never ending unfulfilling task, a task that leads to distress and darkness, a chain that needs to be broken!

Possible Reasons for OCD

Not much research has gone into reasons why people develop OCD, however looking into my past and that of my friends I can see reasons for it. For myself it developed from great anxiety and stress that I put on myself developing bad skin during my teen years, this caused serious stress, and made me feel extremely anxious, especially when around large groups of people, that for me is what triggered my problems and issues.

. . . .

THINK ABOUT YOURSELF and your past, is there one defining moment that has happened to you? Is there some situation or an event from your past that could be the root underlying issue that has then led to you developing OCD? readers please think about this, this may help.

. . . .

TAKE MODERN MEDIA AND the unrealistic images of stars and reality stars, these images of so-called perfection (often digitally enhanced) push the teenage mind to try and keep up, that this is the way to be perfect and look perfect. This can lead to obsession with self-image and a compulsion to keep checking themself to make sure they're fitting this so-called ideal. Life is hard on the young minds in today's world, so much imagery overload with social media fuelling this troubling issue.

. . . .

A SECOND POSSIBLE REASON for OCD is a hereditary issue, new research has shown that people whose parents themselves suffered from OCD have a higher chance of developing it themselves. Look at your parents or other family members, is there any sign of OCD in them? Look towards your kids, is there any sign of OCD in them? Be aware of this, if you see it developing in a family member you will be in a great position to help them before it gets worse, use your own knowledge and apply it to them. Sometimes helping others helps yourself, this can be a really effective way of controlling your own problems.

. . . .

STRESS AT WORK OR AT home can also be a trigger of OCD problems, some people who want to control every aspect of their life can often find themselves falling into the trap of OCD. OCD is about being 'obsessive' so we can see how easy it would be for a controlling person to be susceptible to Obsessive Compulsive Disorder.

You may also have been susceptible to OCD as most people don't often realise they have this problem until something in their life changes like their routine. This could be a job change, relationship change or even a baby, their life turns upside down. Their life is no longer in their full control and they are left with the 'obsessive compulsive' feeling, of needing to regain control of their life in some way, so this big change in their life could be the catalyst, so reader does this sound like you?

. . . .

A FRIEND OF MINE GETS really stressed out over every single little thing and I ask him what are you stressing about and panicking about? he doesn't really know, he says he has this constant anxious feeling within him, almost like being hyper aware of things. I told him sometimes you need to step back and look at what you're really worrying about, is it something about yourself? As a lot of these feelings I think come from a problem with self image or how you think others see you, with me it was the way I looked and what others saw when they looked at me.

. . . .

I STILL SOMETIMES THINK when I'm out *'there really looking at me, Why?, what are they looking at?'*, and in the past this would panic me and stress me, now I just try and let it go, the anxiety is still there but instead of letting it rule me, I rule it!!

. . . .

A GREAT BUDDHIST SAYING is *'sit loose to life'*, and this is so true with dealing with OCD, sit loose, don't question yourself too much, accept your not perfect, and let it go.

Well, I've told you my story, and talked about issues surrounding OCD, I don't expect you to read this and think I'm an expert, but like I said, I am someone with experience with OCD both having it and loving with people who have it, so maybe this kind of does make me in a way an expert.

. . . .

ANYWAY, PLEASE READ this again and understand what you or a loved one is going through, look further on the internet for more information, there are many help groups out there, remember you need to communicate to deal with OCD, don't be alone.

. . . .

'Take your time, there's no rush, breath deeply everyday and don't hold onto negative thoughts'

Well 16 years has passed since I started this book, I'm now 43 going on to middle age noooooooooo! And this book was sat on my old computer and recently found it again and want to add my thoughts and life experiences from the last 16 years, hopefully some nuggets of wisdom will appear, we can only hope right

Getting Older and my OCD Challenges

As I've written I struggled with the way I looked from being a teenager with bad acne. I was always a little shy as a youth but this acne really affected me.

• • • •

THROUGH MY TEENS AND into my young 20's I hid away from people obsessing with the way I looked to others and how others saw me. This went on through my first real relationship and the difficulties with being with a person who had really bad OCD. This led to my marriage and my wife who also suffered from bad OCD. It seems wherever I turned I had this terrible thing in my life called Obsessive Compulsive Disorder, either from me suffering from it or from the person I was with, non stop from the age of 13, crazy isn't it !

• • • •

I NOW HAVE TWO YOUNG children who have just lived through 2 years of lockdown and I mentioned my ex partner suffered greatly from OCD for years and this pandemic pushed her to new levels of distressing mental health. I made sure I kept a close eye on my kids during this time, sometimes I had to talk to them through windows or doors or just over the phone. I always made sure I paid attention to them and if they showed any mental health signs or any OCD signs, I would point it out to my ex or to anyone that would listen.

Sometimes those closest to the problem don't see it so I made sure I was aware of them and how they were coping with being literally locked in a house and garden for nearly two years.

• • • •

OCD IS LIKE SWIMMING upstream, you fight and fight and seem to get nowhere. I've suffered from it and lived with others who have had it badly so I have a unique point of view on both sides. I think this gives me a unique perspective as I can see it from both sides, having OCD and living with it and Also living with others who have OCD then trying to live in their world.

· · · ·

PLEASE TRY TO UNDERSTAND the person who has OCD and have compassion for them as they are trapped and do need understanding more than anything else.

· · · ·

IF YOU HAVE OCD TO any degree remember you're not Alone and there is good help out there. You need to start by 'asking' for help as suffering alone will get you nowhere and only make your life harder.

Well where do i start, i think this will be my last chapter in this life long book that's spanned 30 years of my life.

• • • •

LOCK DOWN CAME AND went and myself and my wife struggled and unfortunately separated. This was an amazingly sad time in my life as I struggled again with myself and who I was. With our two children we decided to be the best co-parents there was and discussed in detail how we were going to bring our children up in a separate environment but also together and let them know we are still a family even though mummy and daddy don't live together now.

• • • •

LIFE DIDN'T TURN OUT this way as incredibly sadly she was diagnosed with breast cancer in 2021 and passed away in 2022. This is a hard thing to put down in words as you can imagine and a lot of the references to people in this book who suffered from OCD badly was her.

• • • •

I SPENT THE WHOLE OF 2022 looking after our two children and have been fortunate to meet an amazing woman called Louise who has helped me along the way and given meaning back into my life.

• • • •

DURING 2022 I SPIRALLED down and my OCD took control again and drove me further and further into a negative self image and this led to drinking an insane amount of alcohol just to numb myself. I used alcohol as a crutch and my OCD kicked in grabbing onto this new obsession. It was easier to live in a haze than live in the real world and my OCD took over. I was drinking whole bottles of vodka, gin, rum and whisky each night and I mean whole bottles.

. . . .

I DRANK MORE THAN SHOULD have been possible and I'm lucky to be here today.

. . . .

I SPENT NIGHTS DRINKING and crying, I would spend a week in a haze of alcohol trying to live a normal life. I drank more than most adults could handle and the only reason I am still here today is I believe it's my size that saved me. I'm 6ft 3in and 18 stone and have always been strong and athletic and I believe this is the reason I'm still alive today.

. . . .

MY BODY TOOK THE DAMAGE I gave it, I know I have damaged myself to some degree but since the end of 2022 I have managed to regain control of myself and curb the drinking and self destruction. I have focused on my kids and embraced Louise who is one of the kindest people I have ever met and has helped me get off my knees and dragged me from defeat to well, lets say im doing a lot better now.

. . . .

IT'S NOW JUNE 2023 and still with struggles I am still here and still fighting all the way. My OCD still appears at times and gives me doubts and makes me second guess myself but I can see it for what it is and am able to separate myself from it. As far as alcohol goes this has been taken into control and I'm focusing more on my mental well being and fitness now.

. . . .

FINALLY

Let me know your thoughts or how you are doing here
ocdadvise@gmail.com
Let's help each other

EMAILS I HAVE RECEIVED

Here are some of the emails I have received, I have named no names but please read them all and understand you're not alone!

'That is really uncanny I think I know the feeling you're talking about. Sometimes I feel like I'm in one of those cartoon sketches where they look through a window and someone on the other side mimics their face in order to trick the person into thinking they're looking at their own reflection. The character scrutinises their reflection, walks away, and then runs back, just to check if it is actually their reflection or someone playing a joke on them'

• • • •

'hi... I know what you mean about how strong the mind is... and sometimes we don't took conscious about it... two years ago I was having a really bad period in my life... a huge depression and I decided took control about that doing things that make me happy... then I discovered yoga... and in that point I learned how powerful and how destructive we can be with ourselves... yoga can be a good help for you... well, is just a little advice I know is not a total solution but I think maybe can help you to be a little be more in control... my best wishes to you... x'

• • • •

'hi, I am 23 years old and is suffering from OCD for ten years, it started when I was in high school. my OCD is getting more severe as time passes by. it distresses me and the people I love. it always hurts me when I cause trouble and distress to the people around me because of OCD. there are times like now, that it leads me to depression. it bothers me so much that I feel helpless, worthless and pathetic, because I cannot carry out simple things or tasks that a normal person can easily do. I always wash my hands countless times, and it always takes me hours when bathing, I do not want to do that or be like that and cause disturbance to the people who sees me but I cannot control myself in doing those things. another thing that makes my situation more sad is because I live in a country that is still not aware of OCD, I do not know anyone who also suffer from this. I don't have a friend, family or relative that has OCD. I feel alone and very sad. my hours are wasted by just lying in my bed worrying about how can I get through this, how can I be normal like the others. I fear holding door knobs, light switches, touching the floor, touching other people's hands, and other peoples things. I do not touch almost everything, I always wash my things and not let other people touch my things. I always carry an alcohol with me when I leave the house or even just inside my room.. I just want to share this to you because I know you understand...'

• • • •

'So much love is written about here. People who don't want to see the people they love suffer, and in turn want to stop their own suffering that is caused by the actions of someone with ocd. How do we build strength to deal with the constant battles of self worth for both people involved.

I was married for 12 years to someone with ocd. I loved him with all my heart and wanted nothing more than to do what I could to make his life better. In the end I learnt how to swing into action when I saw difficult times approaching, and it worked for a long time. Until I fell to pieces, too many friends died within a year through suicide, car accidents and stupid actions, most of their lives were young, I struggled and needed the support of someone.

That wasn't to be. My partner suffered more and became more uncontrolled, more anxious and more demanding expecting more of me. I realised I had made a rod for my own back and tried to see he needed to start to learn how to manage himself. I sort out specialists, books, doctors and support groups, but he wouldn't act upon any of these suggestions.

In the end our marriage failed when I saw life spiralling down, I had 2 boys and they were being affected severely by the stress, my husband's answers were to join with a group of fellow musicians and smoke dope, (his words, it is only a social thing, but someone on medication for depression and ocd, the two don't mix) In the end I had to make a decision to leave or to stay. I wanted life to improve and the only way I saw that happening was to leave.

Ten years later he still causes me great deal of stress, and I can tell when he is struggling with life, I usually cop the abuse. But at least now I can find comfort in my own home. I am still single and find it very difficult to trust anyone with my heart, I gave so much before.'

• • • •

'I have been married for almost 16 yrs. My husband has OCD and it took him going to Prison 2 times to figure out what he had. I went online and researched it and discovered his problem. After determining his problem he has stayed out of trouble. Our marriage can be very stressful at times. I cry a lot of times while I take my nightly bath. I feel so empty sometimes because I feel our marriage is all about him and what he wants or needs. I do not feel like a real person except when I am at work I can be myself. We have a terrible time communicating because he dwells on every word I say and always takes everything the wrong way. I cannot see myself or would want to see myself without him. He is my best friend and worse enemy all in one. I feel so ashamed to even think this way of him. Your story made me cry and I know I am not the only one out there that hurts from a love one with OCD. Thank you for sharing your story.'

. . . .

'hi

I have just read your view on OCD and it really is a refreshing point of view. I have suffered from OCD for around 11 years now since I left school imp now 28 and married with a baby on the way.

I have been to a few doctors over my OCD, and they all have the same old thing to say like they are reading a text book.

my OCD seems to change as I get over certain things, it goes through stages. for example my first signs of OCD were I would touch and re arrange things in my house over and over again scared if I did not someone in my family was going to get hurt or die.

lately it's all about thoughts, like I think of an ex girlfriend or have a dream about a girl and I have to confess it to my wife or

I see someone who reminds me of a girl I know or something
I did with another girl and I'll have to confess it to my wife.

as you can imagine it drives her crazy and really hates it. the
reason I have to confess it is simple my brain tells me if I don't
tell her something terrible will happen to her, which I know is
ridiculous but I feel I have to just in case.

I really enjoyed the way you said to confront your fear, but
my only problem is that my fears in my head maybe years
from now so I don't know if it is working or not as if I think
something bad is going to happen it could be in a year's time
and I will worry about it.

do you have any advice on how to deal with this problem,
I feel that sometimes I have the weight of the world on my
shoulders and feel so sorry for my wife having to live with me
and put up with my crap.

Kind regards'

• • • •

Thank you for this posting, it really helped me allot. I'm back
in the grip of Ocd/major anxiety again after thinking I'd
beaten it and what you said has helped me to understand why
it is back again.

USEFUL LINKS

http://www.ocduk.org[1] - 'OCD-UK is the leading national charity, independently working with and for almost one million children and adults whose lives are affected by Obsessive-Compulsive Disorder (OCD)'

https://www.mind.org.uk[2] - 'One of the most difficult things about OCD is how people perceive it. Intrusive thoughts and compulsions take a greater toll, yet people don't seem to understand that'

https://youngminds.org.uk[3] - 'Having the same distressing thoughts and urges again and again, can be symptoms of Obsessive Compulsive Disorder. Find out more about OCD and what to do if you're affected by it'

---

1. http://www.ocduk.org/

2. https://www.mind.org.uk/information-support/types-of-mental-health-problems/obsessive-compulsive-disorder-ocd/#.WV-W0oTyuM8

3. https://youngminds.org.uk/find-help/conditions/ocd/